Kennedy

PETER CHRISP

HODDER
Wayland

an imprint of Hodder Children's Books

© 2002 White-Thomson Publishing Ltd

Produced for Hodder Wayland by
White-Thomson Publishing Ltd
2/3 St Andrew's Place
Lewes
BN7 1UP

Other titles in this series:
Churchill
Stalin
Hitler

Series concept: Alex Woolf
Editor: Nicola Edwards
Design: Derek Lee
Consultant: Dr John Bourne,
   University of Birmingham
Picture research: Shelley Noronha,
   Glass Onion Pictures
Map artwork: Nick Hawken
Proofreader and indexer: Sue Lightfoot

First published in Great Britain in 2002 by Hodder
Wayland, an imprint of Hodder Children's Books

British Library Cataloguing in Publication Data
Chrisp, Peter
   John Fitzgerald Kennedy. - (20th century leaders)
   1. Kennedy, John F. (John Fitzgerald), 1917-1963
   2. Presidents - United States
   I. Title
   973.9'22'092

ISBN 0 7502 3586 1

Printed in Hong Kong by Wing King Tong

Hodder Children's Books
A division of Hodder Headline Limited
338 Euston Road, London NW1 3BH

Picture acknowledgements: All pictures are from the John
F Kennedy library except: pp 7, 22 Camera Press;
pp14, 17, 28, 33, 49(b), 52, 58 Corbis; pp21(b), 29,
35 HWPL; pp13, 19, 23, 24, 25, 38, 42, 46, 47, 49(t),
53, 54, 55, 56, 57 Popperfoto; title page and pp 15,
18, 21(t), 27, 31, 40, 41, 44, 45, 50 Topham.

Cover picture: Camera Press London.

Contents

CHAPTER ONE

The Young Kennedy

John Fitzgerald Kennedy was born on 29 May 1917, in Brookline, a wealthy suburb of the city of Boston, Massachusetts. John, or Jack, as his family called him, was the second of nine children born to Joseph and Rose Kennedy. Both sides of the family were Catholic and Irish. John's great grandparents had come to Boston in the 1840s, along with 64,000 other Irish immigrants, fleeing poverty and famine.

Joseph Kennedy was a multimillionaire. He had made a fortune in his early twenties, by dealing in the stock market, using ruthless methods which would now be illegal. A typical technique was called 'stock pooling'. Joseph would conspire with a small group of other traders to buy cheap shares in a worthless company. This would encourage others to invest, and the company's share value would rise. Joseph and his fellow conspirators would then sell, taking a huge profit. The other investors were left with shares whose value collapsed. Joseph was also rumoured to have smuggled whisky in the 1920s, when alcohol was banned in the USA.

▼ The Kennedy family in 1938, when John was 21. From left to right: Rosemary, John, Pat, Jean, Joseph, Teddy, Rose, Joe Jr, Kathleen, Bobby and Eunice.

Thanks to their father's millions, the Kennedy children lived a privileged life, surrounded by servants. They went to the best private schools, and had a summer home at Hyannis Port, Massachusetts, and a winter home in Palm Beach, Florida.

However, despite the family's wealth, the upper classes of Boston looked down on the Kennedys. High society was dominated by Protestant families of English descent, who had been in the USA for centuries. They saw rich Irish people as newcomers and upstarts, and were suspicious about where Joseph Kennedy's money came from. Shut out of high society, the Kennedys became close and clannish.

COME IN A WINNER

According to his sister, Eunice Mary, only one thing made John feel strong emotions:

'Jack hates to lose. He learned how to play golf, and he hates to lose at that. He hates to lose at anything. That's the only thing Jack gets really emotional about – when he loses. Sometimes, he even gets cross.'

Joseph Kennedy had encouraged all his children to be competitive and ambitious. As Rose Kennedy recalled, all that mattered was winning:

'Their father would say ... "If you're in a race, do it right. Come in a winner: second place is no good." '

ILLNESSES

From his birth, John Kennedy was a sickly child, suffering from scarlet fever, bronchitis, whooping cough, diphtheria, weak digestion and various allergies. He had been born with one side of his body longer than the other, which gave him severe back problems. When he grew up, he would have to wear a built-up shoe, to stop him walking in a lop-sided way, and sometimes a corset as well, to protect his back. His younger brother, Bobby, later said of him, 'At least one half of the days that he spent on this earth were days of intense physical pain.'

John was intelligent and curious, and loved reading. He stood out from his brothers and sisters because of his cool, detached, unemotional view of the world, which helped him cope with his many illnesses.

▶ Holding a toy truncheon, young John poses shyly for a photograph.

A POLITICAL FAMILY

John Kennedy came from two political families, the Kennedys and the Fitzgeralds. Both his grandfathers were leading Boston politicians, and one of them, John Fitzgerald, had been the first Irish-American mayor of the city. Like almost all Irish Bostonians, they belonged to the Democratic Party.

DEMOCRATS AND REPUBLICANS

The USA has only two effective political parties, the Democratic Party and the Republican Party. Each draws support from different social groups. In the twentieth century, the Republicans were the party of big business, farmers from the western USA, the upper classes and the white Protestant suburbs. The Democrats drew their support from white southerners, urban workers, and minority groups – blacks, Jews, Hispanics, and Irish.

▼ The Harvard student (see page 7).

Although Joseph Kennedy concentrated on making money, he was also politically ambitious. In 1933 and 1936, he gave financial help to Franklin Delano Roosevelt's successful presidential campaigns. President Roosevelt distrusted Kennedy, but rewarded him by making him ambassador to Britain in 1938.

SCHOOL

From 1931-5, John attended Choate, an exclusive private school. He was overshadowed by his older brother, Joe Junior, who was both an academic success and a popular football player. John showed bravery on the football field, but his frailty meant, as one observer said, that 'you could blow him over with a good breath'. In classes, he was easily bored, and got poor marks in every subject except history and physics.

Joseph Kennedy compared the personalities of his sons: 'Joe used to talk about being President some day, and a lot of smart people thought he would make it. He was altogether different from Jack, more dynamic, more sociable and easy-going. Jack ... was rather shy, withdrawn and quiet. His mother and I couldn't picture him as a politician.'

COLLEGE

In 1936, Jack went on to study at Harvard University, and began to take his academic work more seriously. He travelled to Britain in 1939, working for several months as secretary to his father, now ambassador. This was a dramatic time, with the approach of war between Britain and Nazi Germany. On 3 September 1939, when Prime Minister Neville Chamberlain told Parliament that Britain was at war, Kennedy was watching from the public gallery.

WHY ENGLAND SLEPT

Back in Harvard, Kennedy wrote a thesis about Britain's failure to build up its armed forces in the 1930s, when a show of strength might have prevented the war. Britain, like the USA, was a peace-loving democracy, where the government was elected by the people. Kennedy argued that democracies were at a great disadvantage when confronted by a warlike dictatorship, such as Germany. He concluded, 'If you decide that the democratic form is the best, be prepared to make certain great sacrifices.' In 1940, Kennedy's thesis was published as a best-selling book, *Why England Slept*.

▼ A frail 22-year-old John Kennedy follows his father, now ambassador, onto a plane bound from London to Paris. It is 1939, and war is approaching.

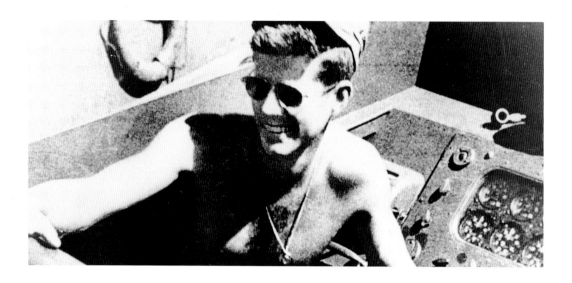

▲ Lieutenant John Kennedy, at the controls of his PT boat. He saw the war as a great adventure.

WAR HERO

By the summer of 1941, it was increasingly likely that the USA would enter the war. John and Joe Jr both joined the navy. Their father used his influence to get John enlisted without a medical examination, which he would certainly have failed with his bad back and poor health.

The USA's war began on 7 December 1941, when the Japanese made a surprise attack on the US Pacific fleet, at Pearl Harbor. John Kennedy, now a lieutenant, volunteered to command PT (Patrol Torpedo) boats – plywood speedboats used to fire torpedoes at Japanese warships. PTs were nicknamed 'bucking broncos' because of the way in which they bounced up and down on the waves, like untamed horses in a rodeo. They appealed to Kennedy because of the excitement they offered. Disliking discipline, he also preferred to command his own boat rather than serve in a junior role on a large warship.

On the night of 1 August 1943, Kennedy was in command of the PT 109 off the Pacific Solomon Islands. In confused circumstances, Kennedy's boat collided with a Japanese destroyer and was sunk, with the death of two crewmen.

Kennedy's carelessness probably caused the wreck, but he showed real heroism afterwards. He led the ten survivors to a tiny island, swimming for five hours with a strap clenched between his teeth, which he used to tow a badly burned crewman. After getting his men safely ashore, he swam back out to sea in a failed attempt to flag down another PT boat. The crew hid for over a week from the Japanese, living on coconuts and rainwater, until they were finally rescued.

Kennedy was awarded the Navy and Marine Corps Medal for 'extremely heroic conduct.' His father made sure that the story was front page news. The *New York Times* headline said, KENNEDY'S SON SAVES 10 IN PACIFIC. John Kennedy himself was slightly embarrassed to be called a war hero. Later asked how he became one, he replied, 'It was involuntary. They sank my boat.'

Joe Jr, a naval pilot, saw his brother's fame as a challenge. To outdo John, he volunteered for an extremely dangerous mission, piloting a plane packed with explosives towards a German target in France. Joe was expected to bail out over the sea, but twenty minutes after take-off, on 12 August 1944, his 'flying bomb' exploded.

▼ Joe Jr in his pilot's uniform, shortly before his death in action.

INTO POLITICS

According to Joseph Kennedy, his eldest son's death meant that John now had to go into politics:

'I got Jack into politics; I was the one. I told him Joe was dead and that it was therefore his responsibility to run for Congress. He didn't want to. He felt he didn't have the ability ... But I told him he had to.'

John Kennedy later recalled to a journalist:

'It was like being drafted. My father wanted his eldest son in politics. 'Wanted' isn't the right word. He demanded it.'

CHAPTER TWO

Candidate Kennedy

CONGRESS

The US legislature (law-making body), called Congress, is made up of two 'houses'. In 1947 the upper house, or Senate, had 96 members, two from each of the 48 states. (Two new states, Alaska and Hawaii, joined the USA in 1959, raising the number of senators to one hundred.) The lower house, called the House of Representatives, had more than 400 members. The number of representatives each state elected varied depending on population size. Massachusetts, where Kennedy stood for office, elected fifteen representatives.

John Kennedy began his campaign to be a Democratic congressman in January 1946. Unlike Joe Jr, he was not a natural politician. He disliked crowds, and was a stiff and nervous public speaker. Yet he overcame his shyness, and worked hard at speech-making. Kennedy's advantages were his good looks, charm, intelligence, war record, and the wealth of his father. Joseph said, 'We're going to sell Jack like soap flakes.' He spent a fortune on advertising, and had 100,000 copies of a newspaper article praising his son's wartime heroism reprinted and delivered to voters.

The candidate also talked about his war record. 'When ships were sinking and young Americans were dying,' he said in one speech, 'I firmly resolved to serve my country in peace as honestly as I tried to serve it in war.'

▶ The new congressman, with his parents and Fitzgerald grandparents.

Kennedy's first campaign was a massive success. He polled 60,093 votes to his Republican rival's 26,007. This was a great achievement for, throughout the rest of the country, the Republicans were winning landslide victories.

JUST WORMS

Between 1947 and 1952, Kennedy was a member of the House of Representatives, serving three terms of office. He hated his time there. Kennedy's main interest was foreign affairs, while the House dealt with domestic issues, which he found boring. Individual representatives had very little power, which frustrated Kennedy. He summed up this period later, saying, 'We were just worms over there.' He was frequently absent from the House on 'fact-finding' trips abroad, and because of ill health.

ADDISON'S DISEASE

Soon after his election, Kennedy fell so ill that he almost died. Doctors discovered that he was suffering from Addison's disease – a failure of the adrenal glands. These glands produce substances, called hormones, which the body needs to fight infection, deal with stress, digest food, and control salt and sugar levels. The disease had gradually destroyed Kennedy's immune system (ability to fight infection) and was making him waste away. Luckily for Kennedy, a new and expensive treatment for the disease, cortisone, had been developed in 1939. Previously, the disease had been fatal.

Regular cortisone injections and pills gave Kennedy back his strength, and made him put on weight. He was left with a weakened immune system, frequently coming down with high fevers. Kennedy claimed these were caused by malaria, caught in the war. As an ambitious politician, he could not admit that he had Addison's disease. Nobody would vote for someone they knew would be in and out of hospital and might well die young. Yet rumours about Kennedy's health would follow him throughout his career.

▲ In March 1948, a sick-looking Kennedy leans on the podium for support while he gives a speech.

11

▲ In 1952, Kennedy, forced to use crutches because of his back, campaigns for the Senate.

SENATOR KENNEDY

In 1952, Kennedy campaigned for the Senate. His opponent, Henry Cabot Lodge, a famous and respected Republican, had beaten his previous Democrat challenger, in 1946, by 330,000 votes. Lodge was expected to win.

The whole Kennedy family took part in an energetic campaign, which was organized by the 26-year-old Bobby. The Kennedy women hosted ladies' tea parties and Joseph spent another fortune on advertising. By election day, John Kennedy had visited 351 cities and towns across Massachusetts. His assistant Francis Morrissey said, 'I'll bet he talked to at least a million people and shook hands with 750,000.' The result was a huge Kennedy victory. As a senator, Kennedy was now a nationally-known figure.

BOBBY KENNEDY

In 1952, Bobby Kennedy (1925-68) had recently graduated from the University of Virginia Law School. He would be John Kennedy's most devoted and trusted adviser throughout his political career. A skilled organizer and a man with immense drive, Bobby could also be aggressive and bullying, traits which made him many enemies. Joseph Kennedy once summed up the difference between his two sons:

'You can trample all over (Jack), and the next day he's there for you with loving arms. But Bobby's my boy. When Bobby hates you, you stay hated.'

◀ Jackie Kennedy was a sophisticated woman, who had studied in Paris, and appreciated art, ballet and classical music.

MARRIAGE

In September 1953, John Kennedy married society beauty Jacqueline Bouvier. The couple had little in common, and marriage did not stop Kennedy chasing other women. Yet the marriage, and the birth of two children, made Kennedy politically more respectable, allowing him to present himself as a settled family man. Jackie's interests in culture also improved Kennedy's public image by giving him 'class'.

BACK OPERATION

In the summer of 1954, Kennedy's health broke down yet again. His back problems grew so bad that he could not walk without crutches. In October he had major back surgery - a very risky procedure to someone with his weak immune system. Kennedy went into a coma and nearly died, yet he pulled through, making medical history as the first Addison's sufferer to survive such a big operation.

PROFILES IN COURAGE

During his long slow recovery, Kennedy worked on a series of short biographies of ten senators he admired, which he published in 1956 as *Profiles in Courage*. The book won the Pulitzer Prize for biography and gave Kennedy a reputation as an intellectual. In accepting the award, Kennedy concealed the fact that much of the actual writing was done by his speechwriter, Theodore Sorensen.

COLD WAR

John Kennedy entered politics at the start of the Cold War, the USA's long struggle with the Soviet Union. It was a contest between two superpowers and two rival political and economic systems: US capitalism, based on the ideals of democracy and the freedom of the individual to own capital, or wealth; and Soviet communism, based on the ideals of equality and common ownership of property. This was the struggle which would dominate Kennedy's political life.

In 1949, the USA suffered a serious setback in the Cold War, when Chinese Communists conquered the whole of mainland China. The following year, communist North Korea, backed by the Soviets, invaded South Korea. To most US politicians, including Kennedy, these events were evidence of a worldwide conspiracy, directed by the Soviet Union.

▼ Demonstrators protest against communists in the USA. In fact, there were far fewer communists than the 'red scare' led people to believe.

RED SCARE

Cold War setbacks led to the rise of a Republican senator from Wisconsin, called Joe McCarthy. In 1950, he claimed that China had been lost to communism because of traitors inside the US government. Without offering any evidence, McCarthy named dozens of government employees as communists. Their careers were all ruined.

This was the beginning of a 'red scare', a fear of communism that was to grip the USA for the next four years. The scare helped the Republicans win their landslide victory in the 1952 election, ending sixteen years of Democratic rule.

After 1952, McCarthy over-reached himself. He foolishly attacked the new president, General Dwight

D. Eisenhower, a popular war hero, for being soft on communism, and claimed that the army itself had been infiltrated by communists. In July 1954, the Senate voted, by 67 votes to 22, that it did not approve of McCarthy's methods.

John Kennedy was the only Democratic senator who did not vote in the motion against McCarthy, pleading his bad back. McCarthy, a fellow Irish Catholic, was a friend of Joseph Kennedy, and a hero to the Irish voters in Massachusetts. Although Kennedy had come to dislike McCarthy's methods, he felt that he could not afford to upset his electors.

LIBERAL DISTRUST

The Democratic Party included many liberals, who were defenders of the civil rights which McCarthy had abused. So they were the strongest opponents of McCarthy.

▲ Senator Joseph McCarthy questions a witness, at his 1954 hearing to unmask communists in the army.

The liberals distrusted Kennedy because of his failure to condemn McCarthy. They felt that apart from personal ambition, he had no strong beliefs. Referring to *Profiles in Courage*, the leading liberal, Eleanor Roosevelt, described Kennedy as 'someone who understands what courage is and admires it, but has not quite the independence to have it.'

Although Kennedy supported many liberal causes, such as measures to fight poverty and improve education, he did not consider himself a liberal. He was a practical politician, who did not want to be linked with one particular group within his party.

POLITICS IS A JUNGLE

In his notes for *Profiles in Courage*, written soon after the fall of McCarthy, Kennedy summed up his practical view of politics:

'*Politics is a jungle – torn between doing the right thing and staying in office – between the local interest and the national interest – between the private good of the politician and the general good.*'

RUNNING FOR PRESIDENT

In 1957, John Kennedy began a three-year campaign to become president of the USA. His first task was to convince his own party that he would be a good candidate. He had major disadvantages. He was a Catholic, in an overwhelmingly Protestant country, which had never elected a Catholic president. He was also young and inexperienced in high office. Unlike most presidential candidates, he had not been a state governor, vice-president, or a leading senator.

▲ Kennedy campaigns for Democratic support in West Virginia.

Kennedy campaigned by travelling all over the USA, making speeches to local Democratic parties, and meeting party leaders. From 1959, he flew in his own personal plane, *Caroline*, bought for him by his father.

PRIMARIES

The party's presidential candidate was chosen at the national convention – a meeting of party delegates from all over the USA. The delegates themselves were selected by their local party leaders, or in regional elections called primaries.

Candidates for the presidency could also win support by competing for votes in primary elections, called 'presidential primaries'. This was a risky tactic, for defeat could end a candidate's chances at an early stage. It was also very expensive, since the candidate would have to pay for campaign expenses, such as advertising. In 1960, only two of the seven candidates chose to fight in primaries: Hubert Humphrey, a leading liberal, and John Kennedy.

For Kennedy, the key primary was that of West Virginia, where 95 per cent of the population was Protestant. Winning West Virginia would show that a Catholic could be elected. If he lost, his campaign for the presidency would be over.

TELEVISION

In West Virginia, Kennedy fought another dynamic campaign. His father spent $34,000 on television adverts, a medium in which Kennedy proved to be a naturally gifted performer. Journalist Theodore White described a typical election broadcast:

'It opened with a cut of a PT boat spraying a white wake through the black night, and Kennedy was a war hero; the film next showed the quiet young man ... receiving the Pulitzer Prize, and he was a scholar; then the young man held his golden-haired daughter of two, reading to her as she sat on his lap, and he was the young father.'

Humphrey was not rich, and could not hope to compete with Kennedy's level of publicity. On 10 May 1960, Kennedy won the primary by 219,246 votes to 141,941. Humphrey withdrew from the presidential contest, saying privately, 'You can't beat a billion dollars.'

Humphrey's withdrawal meant that the liberals in the party now had no effective candidate. Although many still distrusted Kennedy, they decided to back him. He seemed preferable to his main rival, Lyndon Johnson, from Texas. Johnson was an expert politician who had dominated the Senate, but his image was that of a conservative southerner. Kennedy also convinced the party leaders that he was more electable.

In July 1960, in Los Angeles, the Democratic convention chose Kennedy as presidential candidate. Having beaten Johnson, Kennedy asked him to run as his vice-president. Liberals felt betrayed, but Kennedy knew that he would need Johnson to win over voters in the South.

▼ At the Los Angeles convention, Kennedy shakes hands with Lyndon Johnson, whom he had chosen to run as his vice-president.

A NEW FRONTIER

In his speech on being chosen as Democratic candidate, Kennedy spoke about a 'new frontier', a phrase he would constantly repeat throughout the 1960 campaign: 'We *stand on the edge of a new frontier – the frontier of the 1960s – a frontier of unknown opportunities and perils – a frontier of unfulfilled hopes and threats.*'

Kennedy's talk of a 'new frontier' turned his youth and inexperience into an asset. The 1950s had been the era of Eisenhower, who was already 62 when he took office in 1952. Eisenhower was a cautious conservative, who saw the president's role as that of a caretaker. Kennedy criticized this attitude, saying, '*I believe the American people elect a President to act.*' He promised to provide dynamic leadership that would '*get America moving again.*'

KENNEDY AGAINST NIXON

▼ Running for the presidency in 1960, Kennedy attracted huge crowds. He had grown into a strong public speaker.

Kennedy's Republican opponent was Eisenhower's vice-president, Richard M. Nixon. Kennedy was only four years younger than his rival, yet Nixon looked and acted much older. Nixon's campaign was based on his greater experience. He said that, at the height of the Cold War, the USA could not afford to trust an inexperienced man like Kennedy with the presidency.

In September, the rivals met for the first of four debates, which were broadcast on television and radio. They agreed on most issues. Their only real argument was over Kennedy's insistence that the USA was not doing enough to fight communism, and Nixon's claim that it was.

Many radio listeners thought that Nixon, with a deeper voice, sounded more authoritative. But far more people watched the first debate on television, where they saw the sweat streaking Nixon's badly applied make-up, and his stiff, nervous manner. Kennedy, who had a suntan, looked healthy, handsome and confident.

▲ A stiff-looking Richard Nixon (left) waits his turn to speak, in one of the candidates' four television debates.

NARROW VICTORY

The result of the election, on 8 November 1960, was one of the closest in US history. While 68 million Americans voted, Kennedy won by just 118,574 votes. Nixon believed that there had been electoral fraud in some of the key counts. He told friends, 'We won but they stole it from us.' Nixon would nurse his grudge against Kennedy for many years.

At 43, Kennedy was the youngest man ever elected as US president, and the first Catholic.

CHAPTER THREE

President Kennedy

Friday, 20 January 1961, was a bitterly cold day, with snow covering the streets of Washington D.C. Standing on a platform in front of the Capitol building, John Kennedy swore on a Bible 'to faithfully execute the office of President of the United States.' This was his inauguration, a solemn ceremony undertaken by every president since George Washington in 1789.

LET THE WORD GO FORTH

Kennedy gave an inaugural address to the nation, which would become his most quoted speech. It was a Cold War speech, in which he returned to the theme of *Why England Slept* – the cost of defending freedom:

'Let the word go forth from this time and place, to friend and foe alike, that the torch has been passed to a new generation of Americans...

We shall pay any price, bear any burden, meet any hardship ... to assure the survival and the success of liberty...

And so, my fellow Americans: ask not what your country can do for you – ask what you can do for your country.'

▼ President Kennedy gives his inaugural address in Washington D.C.

KENNEDY'S CABINET

Kennedy had spent the two months since his victory selecting his cabinet – the heads of government departments. Remembering that 34 million Americans had voted for Nixon, Kennedy gave two of the most important departments, treasury and defence, to Republicans: Douglas Dillon and Robert McNamara. His main aim was to unite the country behind his leadership.

Kennedy's most controversial appointment was his brother Bobby Kennedy as attorney general (head of the justice department). The president knew that this choice would attract criticism, for Bobby was just 35 and had not even practised law. Kennedy felt that he needed his brother by his side.

NEW FRONTIERSMEN

The historian, Arthur Schlesinger Jr, was appointed special assistant to the president. In his history of the Kennedy years, Schlesinger described the atmosphere in Washington in March 1961, when he arrived to take up his post:

'The New Frontier was in full swing. The capital city ... had come alive... The glow of the White House was lighting up the whole city... A new breed had come to town, and the New Frontiersmen carried a thrust of action and purpose wherever they went.'

▲ The young attorney general, Bobby Kennedy, casually dressed, in his office at the justice department. The Kennedys brought a new informality to American politics.

JACKIE'S WHITE HOUSE

Jackie Kennedy at once began to oversee a complete redecoration of the White House, the president's official residence. At vast expense, she filled it with French antiques and works of art. She organized classical concerts, and hosted parties for famous authors and musicians, such as the composer Igor Stravinsky and the writer André Malraux. The White House was transformed into a centre of culture.

▲ A White House reception, where Jackie is the centre of attention.

CHAPTER FOUR

Fighting The Cold War

It was only after he became president that Kennedy realized the awesome responsibility the job carried. His one previous experience of command had been of a plywood boat. Now he was Commander-in-Chief of the most powerful military nation on earth.

The evening before the inauguration, the departing president, Eisenhower, spent forty-five minutes advising Kennedy about his new job. He began by telling him about 'the Football', the black satchel carried by two military officers, who attended the president at all times. This contained a set of codes which Kennedy would need to give the command to start a nuclear war.

Eisenhower then described the trouble spots around the world, where the Cold War was being fought. He talked of Southeast Asia, where the USA was helping fight two civil wars against communists, in Laos and South Vietnam. He discussed Berlin, the divided city in the heart of communist East Germany, occupied by US and Soviet troops since the end of World War Two. He talked about Cuba, where the communist-style government of Fidel Castro had been established right next to the USA.

▼ Communist guerrillas in Laos set a trap with bamboo spikes.

LAOS

Speaking of Laos, Eisenhower told Kennedy, 'This is the cork in the bottle of the Far East; if Laos is lost to the free world, in the long run we will lose all of Southeast Asia.' This was the 'domino theory', the idea that every country lost to communism was a threat to its neighbours, which would be knocked over like a row of dominoes.

Kennedy believed in the domino theory. However, over the following weeks, he came to the conclusion that Laos was not the place to make a stand against communism. The Laotian Communists, backed by the Soviet Union, were winning the war, and the country, surrounded by hostile neighbours, was hard to defend. Kennedy decided that the place to stop communist expansion was Laos's neighbour, South Vietnam. Unlike Laos, South Vietnam had a long coastline, where the US Navy could bring in supplies, and an apparently strong anti-communist leader, President Diem.

Kennedy quietly pulled out of his commitment to Laos, negotiating a peace deal with the Soviet Union. A 'neutral' government was set up, including Communists. Kennedy knew that this was just a temporary solution, for the new government was too weak to hold on to power.

Kennedy could afford to pull out of Laos because most US citizens did not even know where the country was. They were far more worried about Cuba, the little island just 140 km from the USA. Discussing Cuba, Eisenhower said to Kennedy, 'We cannot let the present government there go on.' Kennedy agreed with him.

▼ Peace Corps volunteers arrive in Pakistan.

PEACE CORPS

The military struggle was only one side of the Cold War. Just as important to Kennedy was persuading poor nations around the world that capitalism was a better system than communism. One of his first acts as president was to announce the formation of a 'Peace Corps' of volunteers, mostly young, who would travel abroad to work in developing countries, as doctors, nurses, teachers and engineers. Kennedy saw his Peace Corps volunteers as ambassadors for the American way of life.

CASTRO

On 1 January 1959, Fidel Castro (1926–) took power in Cuba, after winning a three-year war against Fulgencio Batista, a corrupt and unpopular dictator. Although Castro did not call himself a communist in 1959, he seemed to most US citizens to act like one. He seized the holdings of US big businesses which owned much of the island's industries and farms. When Eisenhower responded by refusing to buy Cuban sugar, Castro turned to the Soviet Union for trade and aid.

Although Castro had promised to restore democracy, he ruled as another dictator. By 1960, this broken promise had cost him the support of thousands of middle and upper-class Cubans, who emigrated to the USA. Yet Castro used his power on behalf of the poor masses of Cuba, building them schools, hospitals and decent homes.

BAY OF PIGS

On being elected, Kennedy was told that a plan was already in place to overthrow Castro, using a force of Cuban émigrés. The plan had been devised by the Central Intelligence Agency (CIA), the government agency responsible for gathering foreign intelligence and organizing secret operations.

The invasion force was tiny, just 1,400 Cubans, which the CIA had been training in Guatemala, in Central America. The success of the operation was partly based on the belief that Fidel Castro was deeply unpopular in Cuba, and that an invasion would set off a general uprising against him.

Kennedy gave his approval to the plan, on the condition that US involvement could be kept secret. He expected to win, for so far he had met with nothing but success in his career.

DISASTER

From the beginning, everything went wrong with the CIA operation, which Castro knew all about, thanks to his spies. On 17 April 1961, when the troops landed at the Bay of Pigs, on the south coast of Cuba, Castro was waiting for them. The only uprising was against the invaders, as thousands of Cubans, led by Castro, surrounded the beachhead. Outnumbered and outgunned, the invaders surrendered after two days.

The invasion might have succeeded if Kennedy had sent in the US Air Force. He refused to do this, despite the pleas of the CIA and the Chiefs of Staff (military heads). Kennedy told them, 'I don't want the United States involved with this.'

Kennedy had suffered his first and greatest defeat. Many remembered Nixon's criticisms of him during the previous year's campaign. Perhaps, as Nixon said then, Kennedy was too inexperienced to be trusted with the presidency.

▲ Some of the 1,189 prisoners, captured by Castro at the Bay of Pigs.

EISENHOWER'S VIEW

On 22 April, Kennedy had another meeting with President Eisenhower, who asked him why he had not backed up the invasion with US air support.

Kennedy: *'We felt it necessary that we keep our hand concealed in this affair; we thought that if it was learned that we were really doing this and not these rebels themselves, the Soviets would be very apt to cause trouble in Berlin.'*

Eisenhower: *'That is exactly the opposite of what would really happen. The Soviets follow their own plans, and if they see us show any weakness that is when they press us the hardest... How could you expect the world to believe that we had nothing to do with it? ... There is only one thing to do when you go into this kind of thing, it must be a success.'*

▶ In June 1961, Kennedy met the Soviet Premier, Nikita Khrushchev, in Vienna. Kennedy was badly shaken by the meeting.

MEETING KHRUSHCHEV

A month after the Bay of Pigs, Kennedy flew to Europe to meet the Soviet Premier, Nikita Khrushchev, in Vienna. Kennedy hoped to build up a personal relationship with Khrushchev, to prevent either of them starting a nuclear war by miscalculation.

Khrushchev knew that Kennedy was young and inexperienced, and suspected that he might also be weak. He was especially confident because, while Kennedy had been humiliated in Cuba, the Soviets had just scored a triumph. On 12 April, the Soviet cosmonaut, Yuri Gagarin, had orbited the earth, becoming the first man in space. Khrushchev decided to use the meeting to test Kennedy.

KHRUSHCHEV

Nikita Khrushchev (1894-1971) was the son of a peasant, born in a mud hut, who had worked his way up through the Communist Party. He could be ruthless, but he was also an idealist who believed that communism was the way forward for all mankind.

BERLIN

Khrushchev's main worry in 1961 was Berlin. The city was in the middle of communist East Germany, yet the Communists only controlled its eastern half. West Berlin was, in Kennedy's words, 'an island of freedom', occupied by US, French and British troops. Their presence was justified because, at the end of the Second World War, in 1945, the winning countries had been unable to agree on what to do with Germany. This meant there had not even been a peace treaty, or a formal agreement to end the war.

The problem for Khrushchev was that each week thousands of East Germans were fleeing to the West, using Berlin as their escape route. If he was to save the East German economy from collapsing, he needed to block this escape route.

At Vienna, Khrushchev demanded that Kennedy sign a peace treaty within six months, recognizing East Germany and giving it control over West Berlin. If Kennedy refused, Khrushchev said that he would sign his own treaty, even if this led to war with the USA. In an attempt to intimidate Kennedy, Khrushchev smashed the table with his hand and cried, 'I want peace. But if you want war, that is your problem.'

TESTING PLACE

Kennedy had to prove to Khrushchev that he was willing to go to war to defend West Berlin. In a television speech on 3 August, he announced a massive increase in military spending and described West Berlin as 'the great testing place of Western courage and will.' He said that an attack on West Berlin would be taken as 'an attack upon us all.'

▲ In August 1961, an East German soldier in Berlin flees to the West. A few days before, the East Germans had begun to build the Berlin Wall, sealing off their half of the city.

BERLIN WALL

At midnight on 12 August, without warning, the East Germans started building a barrier across Berlin, blocking the escape route to the West. The building of the wall caused widespread alarm in West Berlin, where it was seen as a prelude to a Soviet take-over. In fact, as Kennedy realized, it was a sign that Khrushchev had backed down. He said to his advisers, 'Why would Khrushchev put up a wall if he really intended to seize West Berlin? It's not a very nice solution, but a wall is a hell of a lot better than a war.'

OPERATION MONGOOSE

Although the Berlin crisis kept Kennedy busy throughout the summer and autumn of 1961, he had not forgotten about Fidel Castro. His Bay of Pigs humiliation made him even more determined to remove the Castro regime. Bobby Kennedy, who had developed an obsessive hatred for Castro, suggested a campaign of 'espionage, sabotage, general disorder.' Codenamed 'Operation Mongoose', the plan was given the president's approval in late 1961. This was the beginning of an undeclared war against Castro. Cuban agents, trained and armed by the CIA, blew up factories and bridges, set fire to crops, and assassinated Cuban officials.

Fidel Castro was convinced that the sabotage campaign was a prelude to a fresh invasion, and he persuaded Nikita Khrushchev that the Soviets had to do something to defend the island. In April 1962, Khrushchev decided on a bold gamble – he would secretly install nuclear missiles in Cuba. Protecting Cuba was only one of Khrushchev's motives. Just as important was the power that such missiles would give the Soviet Union.

▶ Castro and Khrushchev embrace during their first ever meeting, in New York, in 1960.

THE NUCLEAR ARMS RACE

In the late 1950s, Khrushchev had boasted that Soviet factories were turning out nuclear weapons *'like sausages'*, and that his missiles could *'hit a fly in space'*. Khrushchev was bluffing. Soviet missiles had the range to target Western Europe, but Khrushchev had hardly any effective long-range missiles which might threaten the USA.

Kennedy had fallen for Khrushchev's bluff and, during his campaign to be president, he accused Eisenhower of letting the Soviets get ahead in the arms race, allowing a *'missile gap'* to open.

On becoming president, Kennedy was told by the military that the only missile gap was in favour of the USA. Despite this, Kennedy began the greatest armaments build-up in history. Building weapons was one thing that Kennedy could do to show Khrushchev that he had the guts to stand up to him.

CALLING KHRUSHCHEV'S BLUFF

In response to Soviet threats to seize Berlin, Kennedy decided to call Khrushchev's 'missile bluff' (see panel). On 21 October 1962, the Under-Secretary of State, Roswell Gilpatric, gave a speech in which he announced that the USA had tens of thousands of nuclear weapons, far more than the Soviet Union possessed.

▼ A British cartoon shows Cuba as a tiny storm-tossed boat, caught between the rival superpower leaders.

What Kennedy did not realize was the difficult position that he had placed Khrushchev in. The Soviet Union could not afford to match US military spending, yet Khrushchev was now under great pressure from his own military to catch up with the USA. For Khrushchev, sending medium-range missiles to Cuba was a much cheaper solution than developing new long-range missiles.

Khrushchev also resented the fact that the US had installed missiles in Turkey, close to the Soviet Union. He felt that he had the same right to place his own weapons in Cuba.

CHAPTER FIVE

The Cuban Missile Crisis

On 16 October 1962, Kennedy was given a terrible piece of news. The CIA had been analyzing new photographs of Western Cuba, taken by a U-2 spy plane. These showed that the Soviets were building nuclear missile-launching sites on the island. Once they were completed, they would have the ability to wipe out cities across the USA. Kennedy was furious because Khrushchev had repeatedly assured him that he would not send offensive weapons to Cuba. His first reaction was to say, 'He can't do this to me!'

This was the beginning of the Cuban Missile Crisis, which would bring the two superpowers to the edge of nuclear war. October 1962 would be the most dangerous month there had been in human history.

▼ This map shows the range of the Soviet missiles and bombers being sent to Cuba.

Jet bombers - 1130 kilometres
(Atlanta, Miami, Central America)

Medium range ballistic missiles - 1600 kilometres
(Washington DC, Houston)

Intermediate range ballistic missiles -
3600 kilometres (nearly all of USA)

OPTIONS

Kennedy assembled a team of twenty advisers, later called Ex-Comm (Executive Committee of the National Security Council). Everyone agreed that he had to do something to remove the missiles. Allowing them to stay would be a humiliating defeat for a president who had promised active leadership in the Cold War.

The idea of negotiating with Khrushchev was rejected. This would have given the initiative to the Soviets, and Khrushchev had already shown that he could not be trusted. The Chiefs of Staff urged Kennedy to allow them to bomb the missile bases. It would have to be a surprise attack. A declaration of war would allow the Soviets to conceal the missiles in the Cuban jungle, and then launch a devastating counter-attack.

Bobby Kennedy and Robert McNamara, the Secretary of Defense, were against this military solution. Bobby argued that a surprise attack by a large nation on a small one would discredit the USA around the world. President Kennedy's main worry was that an assault on Cuba would lead to a Soviet counter-attack, perhaps on West Berlin. As McNamara pointed out, 'After we've struck Cuba … how do we stop?'

BLOCKADE

McNamara came up with an alternative tactic – a naval blockade. The US Navy would surround the island, and prevent any Soviet ships bringing in armaments.

On 20 October, Kennedy told Ex-Comm of his decision to impose this blockade. The Chiefs of Staff said that this would be a mistake, as it would give Khrushchev time to complete the building of the sites. But Kennedy refused to change his decision.

▼ In his television broadcast, Kennedy tells the American people the bad news about the missiles.

TELLING THE PUBLIC

On 22 October, Kennedy went on television and told the shocked public about the missiles, and his decision to impose a blockade, which he called a 'quarantine'. 'The cost of freedom is always high,' he said, 'but Americans have always paid it. And one path we shall never choose, and that is the path of surrender.'

31

Khrushchev was horrified by Kennedy's broadcast. His 'missile gamble' had failed in the worst possible way. Far from protecting Cuba, the Soviet missiles seemed likely to provoke a US invasion. He now had the problem of preventing a war, which he could not win, without a humiliating climb-down. In public, Khrushchev condemned the US blockade. Yet on 24 October, the Soviet ships carrying weapons to Cuba turned back from the quarantine line.

On Friday 26 October, Kennedy received a letter from Khrushchev, in which he spoke at length of the horrors of war. Khrushchev wrote that he would not send arms to Cuba if Kennedy promised that he would not invade. The letter did not mention the weapons already in Cuba, but for Kennedy, it was a hopeful sign that war might be avoided.

BLACK SATURDAY

27 October, later nicknamed 'Black Saturday', brought one piece of bad news after another. In the morning, a second message was received from Khrushchev, broadcast over Radio Moscow. The Soviet Premier now demanded the removal of US missiles in Turkey as the price for taking his own weapons out of Cuba. For Kennedy, such a deal was politically unacceptable. It would show the world that he was willing to sacrifice the security of an ally, Turkey, to protect the USA.

Worse news followed in the afternoon. First Cuban anti-aircraft gunners began to shoot at the US spy planes. Then a U-2 spy plane was brought down by a Soviet missile, killing the pilot, Rudolf Anderson. Almost all Kennedy's advisers agreed that he now had no choice. The first shots had been fired. The president had to launch a full-scale invasion of the island.

ONE LAST CHANCE

Despite all the pressure on Kennedy to attack Cuba (see panel above), he decided to try one last time to find a peaceful solution. Without mentioning the Turkish missile demand, he sent a reply to Khrushchev's Friday letter. Kennedy promised that he would not invade Cuba if Khrushchev removed his missiles.

On Saturday evening, Bobby Kennedy visited the Soviet ambassador, Anatoly Dobrynin. He said that the Turkish missiles would be removed eventually, but that no public deal could be made. Bobby stressed that this was Khrushchev's last chance, and warned that the US military was 'spoiling for a fight'. The president could hold them back no longer.

KHRUSHCHEV BACKS DOWN

Meanwhile, Khrushchev felt that he was losing control of events. He was worried by the warlike behaviour of Fidel Castro, who had ordered his troops to open fire on the US planes, and who now urged Khrushchev to launch a nuclear attack on the USA. Equally alarming was the shooting down of the U-2 spy plane, by a Soviet general acting on his own initiative.

When Dobrynin telephoned with news of his meeting with Bobby, Khrushchev got the impression that there was a real danger that the US military might overthrow Kennedy and start a nuclear war. Close to panic, on 28 October, Khrushchev agreed to remove the missiles. The Cuban Missile Crisis was over.

▼ A U-2 high altitude spy plane, designed to take photographs out of reach of enemy guns.

In June 1963, two thirds of the people of West Berlin came out to welcome Kennedy.

'KENNE-DY! KENNE-DY!'

Kennedy's handling of the Cuban Missile Crisis wiped out the memory of his earlier failure, at the Bay of Pigs. He had finally proved that he had the guts to stand up to the Soviets. Nobody was told that he had secretly agreed to remove the missiles in Turkey.

When he made his second presidential trip to Europe, the following summer, Kennedy was hailed as a hero. In West Berlin, on 26 June, he was given the most enthusiastic welcome of his life. Thousands of West Berliners gathered outside the city hall, where he was due to give a speech, chanting 'Kenne-dy! Kenne-dy!'

COME TO BERLIN!

Moved by the welcome he received in Berlin, Kennedy gave one of his most powerful speeches to the cheering crowd:

'There are many people in the world who really don't understand, or say they don't, what is the great issue between the Free World and the Communist world.

Let them come to Berlin!

There are some who say that Communism is the wave of the future.

Let them come to Berlin! ...

Freedom has many difficulties, and democracy is not perfect. But we have never had to put a wall up to keep our people in, to prevent them from leaving us!'

34

◄ Kennedy gazes over the Berlin Wall, into communist East Berlin.

NEW UNDERSTANDING

Although they remained Cold War enemies, the missile crisis helped both Kennedy and Khrushchev come to a better understanding. Each knew that the other was desperate to avoid nuclear war. To prevent misunderstandings which might lead to future conflict, a teleprinter 'hot-line' was installed, linking Kennedy in the White House with Khrushchev in the Kremlin.

One result of this closer understanding was the first agreement to limit the testing of nuclear weapons. In July 1963, Kennedy and Khrushchev agreed to end the testing of nuclear weapons in the atmosphere, though bombs could still be exploded underground. Kennedy, who had done more than anyone to speed up the arms race, was now trying to bring it to a halt. To Kennedy, it made good sense to stop the arms race while the USA was ahead.

OUR COMMON LINK

On 10 June 1963, Kennedy spoke to students at the American University, Washington, D.C., of the need for both sides in the Cold War to end the arms race and work for peace:

'We are both devoting massive sums of money to weapons that could be better devoted to combating ignorance, poverty and disease. We are both caught up in a vicious and dangerous cycle in which suspicion on one side breeds suspicion on the other, and new weapons beget counterweapons...

Let us not be blind to our differences – but let us also direct attention to our common interests... For, in the final analysis, our most basic common link is that we all inhabit this small planet. We all breathe the same air. We all cherish our children's future. And we are all mortal.'

CHAPTER SIX

Kennedy's Domestic Policy

Although foreign crises took up most of Kennedy's time as president, he had also promised to introduce a programme of major social reforms at home. He wanted to attack poverty, and improve healthcare and education. In order to do this, he needed to win support in Congress.

Unfortunately for the president, Congress was dominated by a conservative alliance of Republicans and southern Democrats, who saw many of Kennedy's proposals as steps towards communism. Most of the southern Democrats had been elected with a much bigger popular vote than Kennedy had in 1960. This meant that, although he was their party leader, they felt free to reject his proposals. They claimed that he did not have a mandate for his reforms. A mandate is the authority given to a politician by the people in elections. The more votes a politician receives, the bigger his or her mandate.

DEFEATS IN CONGRESS

In 1961, Kennedy recommended 355 measures to Congress, of which only 172 were passed. Sixteen of twenty-three major laws he proposed were rejected.

Congress rejected two bills aimed at increasing funding for education. His proposal to raise the minimum wage was also defeated, in the House of Representatives, by just one vote. Kennedy was so frustrated when he heard the news that he stabbed his desk with his paper knife. The bill was eventually passed, but in a much weaker form than he had intended.

The president's greatest disappointment was over health. He had hoped to create a system of health insurance for retired people, called Medicare. Paid for by small deductions from wages, Medicare would provide hospital treatment and nursing care for those over 65. In July 1962, Kennedy's

Medicare Bill was defeated in the Senate, by 52 votes to 48. Bitterly disappointed, he went on television and announced that the result was a 'serious defeat for every American family'.

▲ Caroline and John Jr play with their father in the White House.

Despite all Kennedy's lost and weakened Bills, he did not have a bad legislative record when compared with many previous presidents. His predecessor, Eisenhower, had passed even fewer laws. However, Eisenhower had never talked about a 'New Frontier' or promised to 'get America moving'. Kennedy had promised more, and so was thought by many to have failed.

Kennedy never gave up hoping to get his reforms through Congress. He pinned his hopes on the 1964 presidential election. If he could only get elected to a second term with a bigger share of the vote, Congress would be forced to listen to him.

KENNEDY AND CONGRESS

Lyndon Johnson, who succeeded Kennedy as president, was far more effective at passing legislation through Congress. In 1965, President Johnson looked back critically at Kennedy's dealings with Congress:

'No man knew less about Congress than John Kennedy... When he was young, he was always off to Boston or Florida for weekends... He didn't have a rapport with Congress. He didn't have affection for Congress. And Congress felt he didn't know where the ball was.'

BECAUSE IT IS THERE

Kennedy set a specific goal for space exploration – to land an American man on the moon by the end of the 1960s. In a speech in Houston, Texas on the 12th of September 1962, he declared:

'We choose to go to the moon in this decade and do the other things, not because they are easy, but because they are hard, because that goal will serve to organize and measure the best of our energies...

'Many years ago, the great British explorer George Mallory, who was to die on Everest, was asked why did he want to climb it. He said, "Because it is there." Well space is there, and we're going to climb it... '

▲ The seven original astronauts of 'Project Mercury', the first US manned space programme.

INTO SPACE

One Kennedy project which did win the support of Congress was space exploration. Most US citizens saw Soviet cosmonaut Yuri Gagarin's 1961 space flight as a Cold War defeat. For international prestige, the USA had to catch up with the Soviets. In 1962, Kennedy said, 'This is the new ocean, and I believe the United States must sail on it and be in a position second to none.'

Kennedy's usual opponents in Congress, the southern Democrats, enthusiastically welcomed his space programme, which would benefit their electors in the South. Space exploration meant massive investment and thousands of jobs for four southern states: Alabama and Louisiana, where the rockets were built, Florida, where they were launched, and Texas, where the flights were controlled. By the end of Kennedy's presidency in 1963, the USA had successfully launched six manned space flights.

RUNNING THE ECONOMY

Space exploration and the arms race were vastly expensive. Kennedy worried about the effect of these expenses on the economy. He knew little about economics when he took office, and assumed that the most important thing a president could do was to balance the budget – making sure that the government did not spend more money each year than it received in taxes.

On becoming president, Kennedy had surrounded himself with a team of senior academics, to give him economic advice. In 1961, the USA was in a recession – a time of low economic activity and high unemployment. Kennedy asked these advisers what he could do about it. 'You can't just talk to me in abstract terms,' he told them, 'you've got to make it in terms of people.'

The economists told Kennedy that if he really wanted to 'get America moving again', he should cut taxes. This would encourage economic activity by giving people more money to spend and invest. They said that balancing the budget in the short term was unimportant.

Kennedy, who had just asked the American people to accept sacrifices, felt that he could not get away with immediately doing the exact opposite: cutting their taxes. The idea of not balancing the budget went against his basic instincts; although he was a millionaire, he was careful with money, and was often shocked by the amount his wife spent on clothes. Yet he was a good learner, and by 1962, the economists had won him over. At the beginning of 1963, Kennedy sent his tax proposal to Congress – a massive cut of ten billion dollars, spread over three years. Passed by his successor, Lyndon Johnson, Kennedy's tax cut contributed to a US economic boom in the mid 1960s.

▲ Tense moments, as the Kennedys and Vice-President Johnson watch the live broadcast of the first US manned space flight, by Alan Shepard, in May 1961.

The Struggle For Black Rights

▲ Members of the Ku Klux Klan, a white racist organization, parade in Georgia. With their sinister white hoods and burning crosses, they terrified southern blacks.

In the early 1960s, black people were treated as second-class citizens of the USA. The southern states had their own laws enforcing segregation (racial separation). Black southerners were unable to use the better white schools, restaurants, hotels, and even street drinking fountains. In many places, white racists used the threat of violence to stop blacks registering to vote; in Mississippi, for example, only 60,000 of the one million blacks voted. Life was better in the North, but even here blacks did not have equal access to education, housing and jobs.

FREEDOM RIDES

On 4 May 1961, a group of thirteen young men and women, both black and white, boarded two south-bound interstate buses in Washington, D.C. Their plan was to challenge segregation at southern bus stops, waiting rooms, and eating places. The Freedom Riders, as they were called, knew that this was highly dangerous. Their leader, James Farmer, later said, 'When we began the ride I think all of us were prepared for as much violence as could be thrown at us. We were prepared for the possibility of death.'

The violence began outside Anniston, Alabama, where an angry white mob set fire to one of the buses, and attacked the riders. The second group was badly beaten up by another mob in nearby Birmingham, Alabama. Luckily, nobody was killed, and the riders were flown to safety. This was just the beginning of a series of Freedom Rides over the summer of 1961.

KENNEDY'S REACTION

President Kennedy was horrified when he saw the newspaper photograph of the burning bus. He was about to travel to Europe to meet Khrushchev, and found the story highly embarrassing. It damaged the image of the USA abroad. Summoning his civil rights adviser, Harris Wofford, he asked 'Can't you get your goddamned friends off those buses?'

Kennedy knew that segregation was wrong, and was sure that it would eventually disappear. Yet he viewed the struggle for black equality, like everything else, from a practical point of view. Polls showed that 63 per cent of US citizens opposed the Freedom Rides, and Kennedy wanted to avoid any issue which divided the public. He believed that the world struggle with communism demanded greater public unity. Kennedy favoured gradual change, which would keep pace with public opinion.

What Kennedy did not realize was that his own election had raised hopes for change. Black people were inspired by his inaugural speech, in which he promised to 'pay any price' for 'the success of liberty.' They felt that it was their liberty he was talking about.

▲ The Freedom Riders' bus burns in Alabama. When the bus stopped because of a flat tyre, a racist threw a fire bomb through an open window.

NEW IDEAS

Kennedy asked his black adviser, Louis Martin, to explain the rise in civil rights protests:

Martin: *'Negroes are getting ideas they didn't have before.'*

Kennedy: *'Where are they getting them from?'*

Martin: *'From you! You're lifting the horizons of Negroes.'*

'THIS GODDAMNED CIVIL RIGHTS MESS'

When Kennedy talked about civil rights in private, he described the issue as 'this goddamned civil rights mess'. It was not something that he had thought much about before being elected. Apart from his manservant, he knew few black people, and had little understanding of what their lives were really like. Bobby Kennedy later remarked, in words that also applied to his brother, 'I didn't lose much sleep about Negroes, I didn't think about them much, I didn't know about all the injustice.'

Black leaders, such as Martin Luther King Jr, had given their backing to Kennedy in the 1960 election, expecting that he would introduce civil rights legislation –

Kennedy meets black leaders, including Martin Luther King Jr (second from left).

laws banning segregation. In 1961-2, Kennedy was sure that such laws would be defeated by the southern Democrats in Congress. He told the black leaders that they would have to be patient.

THE BASIC QUESTION

In July 1961, a reporter asked the president to give his view of the Freedom Riders. Anxious not to offend southern whites, Kennedy avoided discussing the moral issue of the rides, and would only talk about the legal aspect. He said, 'The basic question is not the Freedom Riders. The basic question is that anyone who moves in interstate commerce [using buses and trains to move from one state to another] should be able to do so freely.'

Black leaders were disappointed by Kennedy's failure to provide strong moral leadership. They felt that it was part of the president's duty to educate the public, and could not understand why Kennedy did not speak out on television about civil rights.

MORAL PASSION?

After meeting Kennedy, Martin Luther King said of him: 'In the election, when I gave my testimony for Kennedy, my impression then was that he had the intelligence and the skill and the moral fervour to give the leadership we've been waiting for and do what no other President has done. Now, I'm convinced that he has the understanding and the political skill but so far I'm afraid that the moral passion is missing.'

MARTIN LUTHER KING

Martin Luther King, Jr (1929-68) was a church minister in Montgomery, Alabama, where in 1955-6, he became nationally famous after organizing a year-long bus boycott – a mass refusal to use the segregated city buses. As founder and head of the SCLC (Southern Christian Leadership Conference), King travelled the country, making stirring speeches denouncing segregation and encouraging blacks to register to vote.

Influenced by the Indian political campaigner, Mahatma Gandhi, King and his followers practised non-violent civil disobedience. Tactics included boycotts and 'sit-ins' in segregated public places. In 1964, King became the youngest person to be awarded the Nobel Peace Prize.

King's home was bombed, and he lived with constant death threats. On 4 April 1968, he was shot dead by a white racist.

THE BATTLE OF 'OLE MISS'

James Meredith was a young black man who had been inspired by Kennedy's inaugural speech to ask himself what he 'could do for his country'. The day after hearing the speech, Meredith bravely applied for a place at 'Ole Miss', the University of Mississippi, in Oxford, Mississippi, which had never admitted a black student. Rejected, he took the university to court, claiming that he had been turned down solely because of his skin colour. The court backed Meredith. However, Mississippi governor, Ross Barnett, declared that he would ignore the verdict, saying, 'We will not surrender to the evil and illegal forces of tyranny.'

On 20 September 1962, Meredith presented himself for admission at the University of Mississippi. He was turned away by Barnett, watched by a crowd of 2,000 white supporters.

Kennedy hoped that the governor could be talked into changing his mind. Bobby Kennedy made repeated phone calls to Barnett, reminding him of his responsibility to uphold the law. Barnett said, 'I won't let that boy into Ole Miss. I will never agree to that. I would rather spend the rest of my life in a penitentiary than do that'.

When it became clear that the Mississippi law officers could not be relied on to protect Meredith, Bobby Kennedy sent 300 federal marshals to Oxford. They managed to get

Meredith into the university, where they found themselves surrounded by thousands of rioters, throwing bricks and stones. Some of the rioters, armed with guns, shot dead a journalist and a bystander, and wounded dozens of marshals. Peace was only restored when the president sent in 23,000 soldiers, who surrounded the university.

The battle of 'Ole Miss' was a turning point in the struggle for black rights. For the first time, Kennedy had been forced to confront the white racists of the South. He had taken sides.

BIRMINGHAM, ALABAMA

The campaign for civil rights intensified in 1963, and with it the scale of violence. In April, Martin Luther King organized his biggest campaign yet, in Birmingham, Alabama, which he described as 'the most segregated big city in the US.' Thousands of blacks and whites, including children as young as six, took part in sit-ins, boycotts and

marches. Birmingham police chief, Eugene 'Bull' Connor, broke up the marches using high pressure fire-hoses, wooden batons and police dogs. The television news carried shocking pictures of police dogs lunging at women and children, and protesters being flattened by fire-hoses.

DECISION TIME

The police violence in Birmingham (see panel above) sickened Kennedy, and persuaded him that the time had finally come to introduce a civil rights bill. He felt that the news coverage meant that there would now be widespread public support for such a measure, in the North at least. As he explained to Martin Luther King, 'Bull Connor's police dogs finally awakened the American conscience and made it possible for us all to move ahead.'

▲ A black demonstrator knocked to the ground by police in Birmingham, Alabama.

SPEAKING OUT

On 11 June 1963, Kennedy spoke to the nation on television about civil rights, and his reasons for introducing his Bill:

'We are confronted primarily with a moral issue... The heart of the question is whether all Americans are to be afforded equal rights and equal opportunities... This nation, for all its hopes and all its boasts, will not be fully free until all its citizens are free.'

This, at last, was the speech that the black leaders had been waiting for. Martin Luther King wrote to Kennedy:

'It was one of the most eloquent, profound ... pleas for justice and the freedom of all men ever made by any President. You spoke passionately to the moral issues involved in the integration struggle.'

▼ Blacks and whites march together in Washington, in support of civil rights.

THE CIVIL RIGHTS BILL

Kennedy's Civil Rights Bill, which he sent to Congress on 20 June, proposed the banning of segregation in public places, such as hotels, theatres and restaurants. It also included measures to reduce racial discrimination in the workplace, and to help schools desegregate.

The president knew that he was taking a big risk. He was hoping to be re-elected in 1964, and this Bill cost him the votes of millions of southern whites. There was no guarantee that the Bill would even be passed. 'This issue could cost me the election,' he told one black leader, 'but we're not turning back.'

46

MARCH ON WASHINGTON

On 28 August 1963, 230,000 civil rights campaigners from all over the country descended on Washington for a march. Kennedy had originally opposed this, thinking that it might damage the chances of his Bill. When it was clear that he could not stop the demonstration, he decided to take over its organization. Bobby Kennedy supervised the details, ensuring that it was peaceful, and that the marchers were welcomed with food and drink. The protest march on Washington was turned into a march in Washington in support of Kennedy's Bill.

▶ King tells the vast crowd, 'I have a dream!'

LET FREEDOM RING!

The vast crowd assembled in Washington inspired Martin Luther King to give his most powerful and emotional speech:

'I have a dream that one day on the red hills of Georgia the sons of former slaves and the sons of former slaveowners will be able to sit down together at a table of brotherhood...

'Let freedom ring from every hill and every molehill of Mississippi! From every mountainside, let freedom ring! When we let freedom ring, when we let it ring from every village and every hamlet, from every state and every city, we will be able to speed up that day when all of God's children, black men and white men, Jews and Gentiles, Protestants and Catholics, will be able to join hands and sing in the words of the old Negro spiritual, "Free at last! Free at last! Thank God Almighty, we are free at last!"'

CHAPTER EIGHT

Vietnam

Civil rights was only one of the major problems facing Kennedy in the summer of 1963. He was just as worried about events taking place on the other side of the world, in South Vietnam, where yet another crisis was unfolding.

On 11 June, the day that Kennedy made his televised civil rights speech, a 73-year-old Buddhist monk, Thich Quang Duc, committed suicide in the centre of the South Vietnamese capital, Saigon. He sat cross-legged on a pillow, while fellow monks poured petrol over him. Quang Duc then calmly struck a match, and set himself on fire. His suicide was photographed by a US journalist, appearing on front pages around the world.

Quang Duc's suicide was a protest against the brutality of Kennedy's ally, the South Vietnamese President, Ngo Dinh Diem. Kennedy was as shocked by the monk's suicide as he had been by the Freedom Riders. 'Who are these people?', he said, 'Why didn't we know about them before?'

THE VIETNAM WAR

Since 1960, the South Vietnamese government, supported by the USA, had been fighting a civil war against the Communist 'Vietcong', backed and trained by the North Vietnamese. In 1961, Kennedy had decided that this was a war which could and must be won. He sent in a steady stream of weaponry and military personnel and by the end of 1962 there were 11,500 US troops in the country. Officially, they were advisers. In fact, many were also combat troops.

Although Kennedy was determined to win, he was just as determined that the war had to be won by the South Vietnamese themselves. He said, *'In the final analysis it is their war.'*

BUDDHIST CRISIS

Victory in Vietnam (see panel opposite) depended on President Diem's ability to win the support of the population. Unfortunately, Diem seemed to be more interested in using his troops against his own people than against the Communists. Diem was a Catholic, in a land where most of the population was Buddhist. He distrusted Buddhists, and banned their custom of displaying flags on the Buddha's birthday. On 8 May 1963, when thousands of demonstrators protested against the ban, Diem's soldiers fired into the crowd, killing nine people and wounding many others. It was in protest against this action that the Buddhist monk set fire to himself.

▲ A Buddhist monk burns himself to death in Saigon.

Much of the blame for Diem's anti-Buddhist policies lay with his brother and chief adviser, Ngo Dinh Nhu, who was the head of the secret police. Nhu's beautiful and bloodthirsty wife was another embarrassing problem. Madame Nhu fascinated US journalists, who nicknamed her 'the dragon lady' and quoted her outspoken views at every opportunity. Her reaction on hearing of the monk's suicide was typical. She told the journalists that she had clapped her hands in glee when she heard the news, and offered a box of matches for the 'next barbecue'.

▶ Madame Nhu, the 'dragon lady' of Vietnam, at one of her press conferences.

A DEEPENING CRISIS

In the summer of 1963, Kennedy was too busy dealing with civil rights problems to give much attention to the growing crisis in Vietnam. Adding to his difficulty was the conflicting advice he received. Some of his advisers said that the only hope of winning the war lay in getting rid of Diem, while others argued that without Diem, the country would slide into chaos.

Kennedy tried to put pressure on Diem to sack his brother Nhu, and end his anti-Buddhist policies. Diem, a proud man who bitterly resented US interference, refused. On 21 August 1963, Nhu launched an attack on the Buddhist pagodas (temples), destroying holy statues and arresting thousands of Buddhists. In protest, several more monks committed fiery suicide.

Following the attack on the pagodas, a group of South Vietnamese generals approached the US ambassador in

▼ President Diem inspects disarmed Vietnamese paratroopers in November 1960. They had taken part in an unsuccessful attempt to overthrow him.

Vietnam and asked how Kennedy would react if they were to overthrow Diem. Kennedy reluctantly gave them his backing.

On 2 November 1963, the generals moved against Diem, who was arrested with his brother Nhu. Both of them were murdered. Kennedy was at a meeting with his National Security advisers when he heard the news. He turned pale with shock, and hurriedly left the room. General Maxwell Taylor, who had been a supporter of Diem, said, 'What did he expect?'

KENNEDY'S JUSTIFICATION

On September 9 1963, Kennedy gave a television interview in which he used the 'domino theory' (see page 22) to justify continued US involvement in Vietnam: *'China is so large, looms so high just beyond the frontiers, that if South Vietnam went, it would not only give them an improved geographical position for a guerrilla assault on Malaya, but would also give the impression that the wave in the future in Southeast Asia was China and the Communists.'*

KENNEDY'S MISTAKES

Kennedy mistakenly believed that communist countries belonged to a single bloc, and that the Vietcong were controlled by the Chinese. In fact, the Vietnamese Communists were nationalists, who distrusted the Chinese and later went to war with them. With hindsight, we can see that the 'domino theory' too (see page 22) was mistaken.

Kennedy was also mistaken in believing that the generals who overthrew Diem could win the war in Vietnam. They soon fell from power, as did the seven successive military governments which followed.

WHAT WOULD KENNEDY HAVE DONE?

Several of Kennedy's aides believed that he was planning to withdraw from Vietnam following his reelection in 1964. Others, including General Taylor and Vice-President Lyndon Johnson, thought that he would stop at nothing to win the war. Asked what Kennedy would have done, Taylor replied, 'Let me just say this, Kennedy was not a loser.'

We have no way of finding out the truth. Just three weeks after Diem's murder, Kennedy was dead himself.

CHAPTER NINE

Into Nut Country

In late 1963, Kennedy began to concentrate on his campaign for a second term as president. Although he had lost much white support in the South, he was still in a good position to win, for the Republicans had no strong presidential candidate. Kennedy was looking forward to the 1964 election, hoping that he would finally win a popular mandate to get his legislation through Congress.

In November, John and Jackie Kennedy set off on a tour of Florida and Texas. His aims were to raise funds for the coming campaign, and to recover southern support.

On 22 November, the day he was due to visit Dallas, Kennedy woke up in the Texas Hotel, Fort Worth, where he saw a copy of that day's Dallas Morning News. It carried a full-page black-bordered advert attacking him for being pro-communist. Kennedy said to his wife, 'We're heading into nut country today.'

WANTED
FOR
TREASON

THIS MAN is wanted for treason

THIS MAN is wanted for treason

THIS MAN is wanted for treasonous activities against the United States:

1. Betraying the Constitution (which he swore to uphold): He is turning the sovereignty of the U.S. over to the communist controlled United Nations. He is betraying our friends (Cuba, Katanga, Portugal) and befriending our enemies (Russia, Yugoslavia, Poland).
2. He has been WRONG on innumerable issues affecting the se-

3. He has been lax in enforcing Communist Registration laws.
4. He has given support and encouragement to the Communist inspired racial riots.
5. He has illegally invaded a sovereign State with federal troops.
6. He has consistently appointed Anti-Christians to Federal office: Upholds the Supreme Court in its Anti-Christian rulings. Aliens and known Communists abound in Federal offices.

▲ On the eve of Kennedy's visit to Dallas, local right-wingers distributed this 'wanted for treason' handout.

HATE CAPITAL

In 1963, Dallas, Texas, was known as the 'hate capital' of the South. It was a violent city, with one of the highest murder rates in the country. Dallas was a stronghold of extreme right-wing groups, who thought that Kennedy was soft on communism. Just four weeks before the President's visit, Adlai Stevenson, the US ambassador to the United Nations, had been jostled and spat at by Dallas demonstrators. Stevenson warned Kennedy's advisers:

'There was something very ugly and frightening about the atmosphere... I talked with some of the leading people out there. They wondered whether the President should go to Dallas, and so do I.'

DRIVING INTO DALLAS

After flying to Dallas, the Kennedys got into an open car with Governor John Connally and his wife, and set off in a motorcade towards the city centre. Against expectations, most of the people lining the streets cheered and waved flags. Mrs Connally said, 'Well, Mr President, you can't say there aren't some people in Dallas who love you.'

At about 12.30, the motorcade entered Dealey Plaza, a wide-open space overlooked by tall buildings. Moments later, a loud crackle of rifle shots echoed across the Plaza. Kennedy was hit twice, in the neck, and in the back of the head.

The car raced to the Parkland Memorial Hospital, where doctors made a desperate but unsuccessful attempt to save the President's life. At 1 pm, John Fitzgerald Kennedy was declared dead.

▲ Kennedy smiles at the Dallas crowd, moments before his assassination.

THEY HAVE SHOT MY HUSBAND

In 1964, Jackie Kennedy told the Warren Commission, set up to investigate the assassination, about the shooting:

'I heard these terrible noises ... and all I remember is seeing my husband, he had this sort of quizzical look on his face, and his hand was up... I remember thinking he just looked as if he had a slight headache... And then he sort of... put his hand to his forehead and fell in my lap. And then I just remember falling on him and saying, "Oh, no, no, no," I mean, "Oh, my God, they have shot my husband."'

▲ When Lee Harvey Oswald was confronted with this picture he said, 'That picture is not mine, but the face is mine. The picture has been made by superimposing my face.'

WHO KILLED KENNEDY?

Dallas police hunting for the president's killer began to search the Texas School Book Depository, overlooking Dealey Plaza. An eyewitness had seen a man fire a rifle from the sixth floor.

At about 1.15 pm, in South Dallas, police officer J. D. Tippit was shot dead by a man he had stopped for questioning. The gunman then fled to a cinema, where he was arrested after a short struggle. He identified himself as Lee Harvey Oswald, an employee of the book depository.

Meanwhile the policemen searching the depository found a mass of evidence pointing to Oswald as the killer. This included the rifle, used to shoot Kennedy, which had Oswald's palm prints and fibres from his shirt on it. Further investigation showed that the rifle had been bought by Oswald. The police then discovered a photograph of him holding an identical rifle. Oswald denied everything. When he was asked by journalists if he had shot the President, he said, 'No ... I'm just a patsy!'

WHO WAS LEE HARVEY OSWALD?

After a troubled childhood, Lee Harvey Oswald (1939-63) enlisted at seventeen in the US marines, where he became interested in communism. In 1959, he defected to the Soviet Union, marrying a Russian wife, Marina. Disillusioned with the Soviet system, in 1962 he returned to the USA, and made several desperate attempts to defect to Cuba. According to Marina, 'He was the kind of person who was never able to get along anywhere he was.'

Asked why Lee might have wanted to kill the president, Marina said, 'He wanted in any way, whether good or bad, to do something that would make him outstanding, that he would be known in history.'

The day after the assassination, Oswald was being taken through the basement of the Dallas police headquarters, to be transferred to the local jail. Filmed by television cameras, a man called Jack Ruby pushed his way through the crowd, and shot Oswald from close range, killing him. This was the first televised murder in history.

◀ Lee Harvey Oswald, shot dead on live television by Dallas nightclub owner, Jack Ruby.

CONSPIRACIES?

The Warren Commission concluded that Oswald killed Kennedy, acting alone. Yet his death in police custody suggested to many that the assassination was the work of a powerful conspiracy, and that Oswald had been killed to stop him talking. In a 1964 book, *Oswald: Assassin or Fall Guy?*, Joachim Joesten argued that Oswald had been framed by the true culprits – the FBI, the CIA, and a group of rich Texan oil men. This was the beginning of a vast 'Kennedy assassination' industry. Since 1964 hundreds of books have been published, suggesting many different conspiracies. Despite all this research, no proof of a conspiracy has ever been discovered. Yet today, 80 per cent of US citizens believe that Kennedy was killed by a conspiracy.

CHAPTER TEN

Kennedy's Legacy

▼ Kennedy's funeral procession heads for the Capitol building, where his coffin was put on display.

Millions of US citizens can still remember where they were when they heard the news of Kennedy's death. The shock was also felt around the world. Nikita Khrushchev wept when he was told. In France, Charles de Gaulle said, 'They are crying all over France. It is as though he were a Frenchman.' Thousands of West Berliners put candles in their darkened windows. In Cuba, Fidel Castro said, 'This is bad news ... they will try to put the blame on us.'

In death, Kennedy was more popular than he had ever been as a living president. In 1964, the wave of sympathy towards the dead president helped Johnson pass Kennedy's Civil Rights Bill, and then win a crushing victory in the presidential election. Johnson won by fifteen million votes. With the biggest popular mandate ever given a president, Johnson was able to get one liberal measure after another passed, including Kennedy's Medicare legislation and measures to fight poverty and improve education.

KENNEDY LIVES ON

On 27 November, Lyndon Johnson gave his first speech as president, promising to continue the work of Kennedy:

'My fellow Americans. All I have I would have given gladly not to be standing here today. The greatest leader of our time has been struck down by the foulest deed of our time. Today John Fitzgerald Kennedy lives on in the immortal words and works that he left behind... And now the ideas and the ideals which he so nobly represented must and will be translated into effective action.'

◀ Standing beside Jackie, still in shock, Lyndon Johnson is sworn in as the 36th US president. This ceremony took place on the presidential plane at Dallas airport, just hours after Kennedy's assassination.

Johnson also continued Kennedy's space programme. One of his first acts was to rename the rocket launch base at Cape Canaveral, Florida, the John F. Kennedy Space Center. The result of the programme was the fulfilment of Kennedy's promise to land a man on the moon by the end of the decade.

Despite these successes, Johnson's presidency was damaged by another of Kennedy's legacies, the Vietnam War. Johnson stepped up US involvement, attacking North Vietnam with the largest aerial bombardment in history, and sending hundreds of thousands of young Americans to fight in the jungle. By the end of 1966, the USA had suffered 33,000 casualties, and was no closer to winning. At home, there were mass protests against an increasingly unpopular war.

Race was another issue tearing the USA apart. The 1968 murder of Martin Luther King sparked black riots in cities across the country. The country was more divided than ever.

Would things have been any different if Kennedy had lived? Many believe that he might have avoided Johnson's mistakes. Yet Johnson was advised by the same men who had advised Kennedy, and all of them favoured increased US involvement in Vietnam.

A scene from *Camelot*, the stage musical which became linked with the Kennedys. Richard Burton played King Arthur with Julie Andrews as his queen, Guinevere.

CAMELOT

A week after Kennedy's death, his widow phoned Theodore White, a journalist from *Life* magazine, and asked him to write an article about her husband. Jackie, worried about how he would be remembered, asked White to save Kennedy 'from the bitter old men who write history'. She said that history belonged to heroes, and John F. Kennedy should be remembered as a hero.

Jackie told White that her husband had been a fan of the hit stage musical *Camelot*, telling the romantic story of King Arthur and his magical court. According to Jackie, his favourite line was the title song's, 'Don't let it be forgot that once there was a spot, for one brief shining moment that was known as Camelot.' In his article, White argued that, like King Arthur's Camelot, Kennedy's presidency should be remembered as 'one brief shining moment' in American history.

PROMISE

In the 1960s, several members of the Kennedy White House wrote memoirs, in which they presented the late president as a perfect hero. His secretary, Evelyn Lincoln, described Kennedy as a figure of hope and promise:

'He was a promise that all of us might lead a better life in peace. He was a promise that excitement and courage must be central in our lives. He was a promise that we could expect more from ourselves, and that we were better than we knew.'

The idea of the Kennedy White House as a second Camelot caught the public imagination. Not long after, during a Chicago production of the musical, members of the audience wept when the actor playing King Arthur sang Kennedy's favourite line.

ASSESSING KENNEDY

From the 1970s, there was a reaction against the heroic view of Kennedy, as new biographies revealed that he had been less than perfect. The public learned that he had hidden the dreadful state of his health; and that, far from being a faithful husband, he had had affairs with dozens of women. Some writers argued that Kennedy's moral shortcomings made him unfit to have been president at all.

Historians are still sharply divided in assessing Kennedy. His defenders point to his skill at dealing with crises, and the cool head he first showed when he saved his men from the PT boat wreck. Critics argue that many of the crises, like that wreck, were Kennedy's fault to begin with.

A CHANGED MAN

John F. Kennedy changed and grew in the presidency. The inexperienced president of 1961, responsible for the Bay of Pigs disaster, was a different man from the international statesman and campaigner for civil rights of 1963. His greatest enemy, Fidel Castro, on hearing that he had been shot, but not killed, told a journalist:

'Kennedy ... still has the possibility of becoming, in the eyes of history, the greatest President of the United States, the leader who may at last understand that there can be coexistence between capitalists and socialists... Personally, I consider him responsible for everything, but I will say this: he has come to understand many things over the past few months.'

1946
18 JUNE
Elected to the House
of Representatives

1952
4 NOVEMBER
Elected to the Senate

1953
12 SEPTEMBER
Marries Jacqueline Bouvier

1954
OCTOBER
Undergoes a major
back operation
DECEMBER
Senate votes to condemn
Joseph McCarthy

1955
FEBRUARY
Second major back operation

1956
Kennedy's second book,
Profiles in Courage, is published

1959
I JANUARY
Fidel Castro comes to power
in Cuba

1957
27 NOVEMBER
Birth of a daughter,
Caroline Kennedy

1958
4 NOVEMBER
Re-elected by a million votes
to a second term as senator

1960
2 JANUARY
Announces he intends to run
for president
13 JULY
Chosen as Democratic
candidate at the Los
Angeles convention
15 JULY
Kennedy chosen as Democratic
presidential candidate
26 SEPTEMBER
First of four television debates
with Richard Nixon
8 NOVEMBER
Elected president
25 NOVEMBER
Birth of a son, John
Kennedy Jr

1917
29 MAY
Birth of John
Fitzgerald Kennedy

1931–5
Studies at Choate School

1936–40
Studies at Harvard University,
travelling to Europe in 1939

1940
Publication of *Why England
Slept,* Kennedy's first book

1941–5
Kennedy serves in the US
Navy, fighting in World
War Two

1944
12 AUGUST
Joe Kennedy Jr killed in action

1961
20 JANUARY
Takes office and gives inaugural
speech in Washington
I MARCH
Announces setting up of the
Peace Corps

23–26 JUNE
Kennedy visits Berlin and
makes 'Let them come to
Berlin!' speech (24 June)
25 JULY
Nuclear test ban treaty agreed
in Moscow
28 AUGUST
Civil rights march on
Washington
Martin Luther King makes his
'I have a dream' speech
2 NOVEMBER
President Ngo Dinh Diem
overthrown and murdered in
South Vietnam
22 NOVEMBER
John Kennedy assassinated in
Dallas, Texas

1968
4 APRIL
Murder of Martin Luther
King Jr

1969
20 JULY
Astronaut Neil Armstrong
takes first steps on the moon,
fulfilling Kennedy's pledge

12 APRIL
Soviet cosmonaut, Yuri Gagarin,
makes first manned space flight
14-19 APRIL
Failed invasion of Cuba at
the Bay of Pigs
4 MAY
Beginning of the
Freedom Rides
5 MAY
Alan Shepard makes first US
manned space flight
25 MAY
Announces plan to land an
American on the moon by the
end of the 1960s
30 MAY–6 JUNE
Kennedy visits Europe, meeting
Khrushchev in Vienna
11 AUGUST
Decides to increase US help
to South Vietnam
12 AUGUST
Communists build Berlin Wall
OCTOBER/NOVEMBER
Kennedy gives approval to
'Operation Mongoose', a secret
plan to topple Castro

1962
7 JUNE
Announces plan to cut taxes
25 SEPTEMBER–
1 OCTOBER
Riots in Oxford, Mississippi,
when James Meredith becomes
the first black man to enrol at
the University
15–28 OCTOBER
Cuban Missile Crisis

1963
3 APRIL
Martin Luther King begins
Birmingham civil
rights campaign
10 JUNE
Kennedy gives peace speech at
the American University
11 JUNE
Kennedy gives television speech
about civil rights
A Buddhist monk sets himself
on fire in South Vietnam
20 JUNE
Sends Civil Rights Bill
to Congress

ambassador The highest-ranking official representing his or her government in a foreign country.
armaments Military weapons and equipment.

Bill A draft of a proposed law, which is then either passed, rejected, or altered by Congress.
blockade Surrounding a place, such as an island, with ships or troops, to stop supplies, troops or weapons, getting through.

candidate Someone standing for election.
capitalism Economic system based on free enterprise and the right to own individual property.
Capitol Building in Washington where Congress meets.
CIA US Central Intelligence Agency, set up in 1947 to gather intelligence and conduct espionage in other countries.
civil rights People's legal rights as citizens, such as the right to vote, and to have equal opportunities in education and work.
clannish Closely united and suspicious of outsiders.
Cold War Conflict between the USA and its allies and the Soviet Union and its allies, which lasted from 1945 until 1991.
communism Economic system that aims at abolishing private property and creating a classless society.
Congress US law-making body, made up of the House of Representatives and the Senate.
Congressman A member of Congress, especially the House of Representatives. Members of the Senate are called Senators.
conservative Opposed to changing the existing system.
corset A stiff, close-fitting undergarment, worn around the waist.

cosmonaut Soviet name for an astronaut (space traveller).

delegate Someone given the power to act on behalf of someone else. Regional party members choose delegates to vote for them at national conventions (meetings).
democracy Rule by the people, who are able to choose their government in elections, or who vote to make important decisions.
Democratic Party One of the two main US political parties. The Democrats draw support from poorer voters, and are usually more liberal than the Republicans.
desegregate End the enforced separation of blacks and whites.
destroyer A fast warship, designed to protect other ships.
dictatorship Government by a single all-powerful leader (a dictator) or political party.
diphtheria A serious disease caused by a germ which attacks the throat, producing a poison which circulates in the blood.

electoral fraud Cheating during an election, such as voting more than once, or lying about the number of votes counted.
émigrés Those who leave their native country and live abroad. This French word is used, rather than 'emigrants', for those who leave for political reasons. It dates from the French Revolution.
enlist Join the armed forces.
espionage Spying.
Ex-Comm Executive Committee of the National Security Council.

governor An official elected or appointed to rule an area such as a state. Each US state elects its own governor.
guerrilla assault An attack using guerrillas – small bands of soldiers, each acting on its own.

Hispanic Spanish-speaking.

immigrants People who arrive from abroad to settle. In their original homeland, people who leave are called 'emigrants'.
inaugural address Speech given by someone during an inauguration, a ceremony on taking office.
integration Bringing together to form a united whole, in particular, bringing races together.
interstate From one US state to another.

key counts (primaries) In an election contest in which neither party enjoys a huge majority, the districts which are most closely balanced between each side are most important in deciding the final winner. These are the 'key counts'.

landslide victory A win in an election by a vast number of votes.
legislative record Achievement in making laws.
liberal A word with several meanings, including 'broad-minded'. In the 1960s, liberals wanted to build a more just and equal society, through government action to help the poor and underprivileged.
lieutenant An officer in the armed forces, below the rank of a captain.

mandate Political authority, thought to be handed over by people to the politicians they elect. If a politician in favour of lowering taxes is elected by a massive number of votes, he has a mandate for lowering taxes. If he narrowly scrapes in, he has no such mandate.
marines Soldiers who serve on ships, trained to fight on land and at sea.
minimum wage The smallest amount a company is allowed by law to pay workers in wages.
motorcade A procession or parade of motorcars.

nationalists People devoted to their nation, who want to make it more powerful than other nations, or who campaign to free it from foreign rule.

Nazi Germany Germany between 1933 and 1945, when the country was ruled by the Nazi Party led by Adolf Hitler.

Nobel Peace Prize Prize given to someone each year for contributing to peace. This is one of the prizes, along with those for literature and the sciences, set up by the Swedish businessman and scientist, Alfred Nobel. Winners must have helped humankind in an important way.

party leader One of the leading figures in a political party. They include the leaders in Congress, the governors of states, or the mayors of major cities.

patsy Someone framed, or set up to take the blame for something they have not done.

penitentiary A prison.

primary An election staged by a political party, in which the ordinary party members vote to choose candidates for office.

public gallery A balcony or upper floor of seats for the public.

rapport A good and easy relationship. People with a rapport with each other can communicate well, without misunderstandings.

Republican Party One of the two main US political parties. The Republicans draw support from big business and are usually more conservative than the Democrats.

right-wing Right-wingers oppose government attempts to make society more equal and fair, believing that people should accept responsibility for their own lives.

sabotage Deliberately causing damage, such as blowing up buildings and wrecking machinery. Unlike a bombing raid, sabotage is done secretly by agents working inside an enemy country.

segregation Enforced separation of races. Until the early 1960s, US whites and blacks were segregated, particularly in the South.

School Book Depository A storehouse for books to be used in schools.

socialists Socialists believe that the community as a whole should control the economy. They believe that this will make society more equal and fair.

social reforms Measures to make society better, by removing unjust practices, such as segregation.

Soviet Union Name of the former Russian Empire under Communist rule, from 1922 until 1991.

teleprinter Machine for sending and receiving messages by telegraph (electronic signals sent by wire).

term of office The length of time an official is elected to serve.

thesis A long detailed work, written by university students, or a particular argument set down.

torpedoes Cigar-shaped missiles, fired through water.

tyranny Harsh and unreasonable rule.

United Nations Worldwide grouping of countries set up in 1945, at the end of the Second World War, to prevent future wars.

Vice-President The deputy to the US President, who stands in for him if he is unable to perform his duties for any reason. He takes over if the President dies in office, or is removed for misconduct.

FURTHER INFORMATION

BOOKS

Peter Chrisp, *The Cuban Missile Crisis*, Hodder Wayland, 2001

Nigel Hamilton, *JFK: Reckless Youth*, Random House, 1992
A detailed account of Kennedy's youth, ending at the start of his political career. Hamilton presents Kennedy as a flawed figure, though the real villain of the book is Joseph Kennedy Senior.

Seymour Hersh, *The Dark Side of Camelot*, Harper Collins, 1998
A hostile biography, which presents everything that Kennedy did in a negative light.

Richard Reeves, *President Kennedy: Profile of Power*, Papermac, 1994
A gripping, day-by-day account of the Kennedy presidency, showing both his strengths and weaknesses.

WEBSITES

John F. Kennedy Library
The web site of the library run on behalf of the Kennedy family
http://www.pbs.org/wgbh/amex /presidents/nf/resource/ken/ resource/.htm

The Kennedy Assassination Homepage
A superb website, which aims to debunk the mass of disinformation surrounding Kennedy's death, but also provides links to dozens of conspiracy sites. Read the evidence, and make up your own mind!
http://mcadams.posc.mu.edu/ home.htm

14 Days in October: The Cuban Missile Crisis
A lively interactive website on the crisis
http://library.thinkquest.org/ 11046/